Our World

Bath New York Singapore Hong Kong Cologne Delhi Melbourne

Author: Steve Parker

First published by Parragon in 2009
Parragon
Queen Street House
4 Queen Street
Bath BA1 1HE, UK

ISBN 978-1-4075-7189-8
Printed in China

Contents

The houses we live in

Around the world, people live in very different kinds of houses and homes. Some people live in high-rise city apartment buildings, others in tents made of felt.

High homes

Cities are often very crowded, so many people live in flats or apartments. Some of these are in very tall buildings. Hundreds of people may live in one apartment building.

Homes on sticks

In some parts of South East Asia, people build houses held up by strong wooden posts. This keeps the house clear of floods – and snakes. It also helps keep the house cool.

4

Keeping cool

In hot countries, houses have plenty of shady areas to help people stay cool. Houses are often painted white. The white walls reflect, or throw back, the heat of the Sun.

Mobile homes

Some people do not live in one place all the time. They are called nomads. Nomads usually live in tents that they can take down and carry. The nomads of Mongolia live in round tents called yurts. Yurts have a wooden frame, covered in felt, canvas and cotton.

Mud houses

In Africa, houses are often made of mud. The mud can be spread over a framework of sticks and allowed to dry. But the mud can also be used to make bricks. It is pressed into brick-shaped boxes and dried in the sunshine.

5

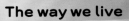

Our clothes

Clothes may keep us warm or cool. Some clothes are very comfortable, others are smart or beautiful. Clothes can show that we belong to a particular group such as a school or a sports team.

Shimmering sari

This beautiful silk dress comes from India. It is called a sari. It is one long piece of material that wraps around the body several times and drapes over the shoulder.

Did you know?

Silk is made by silkworms. These are really caterpillars of the silk moth. They spin a casing, or cocoon, of silk to protect themselves before changing into moths.

Blue jeans

Jeans were created in the USA more than 100 years ago. They are usually made from a strong blue material called denim. Jeans were designed as work trousers for miners.

Bright colours

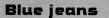

In many African countries the clothes are often brightly coloured. They also have beautiful patterns and special stitching called embroidery. African clothes are usually loose and flowing, to keep people cool in the hot sunshine.

Stay cool

For thousands of years, in the hot Middle East, people have worn long, loose robes. The robes are often white, to 'bounce back', or reflect, the heat of the Sun.

At school

In most countries, children are allowed to go to school all year round. But some children have to stop school at certain times of the year to help gather crops from the fields.

School clothes

In many schools, all the children wear the same kind of clothes as each other, called a uniform. This makes them feel part of the group.

Outdoor school

In countries where it is hot, or the people are poor, school is held out in the open. The children may even sit on the hard ground.

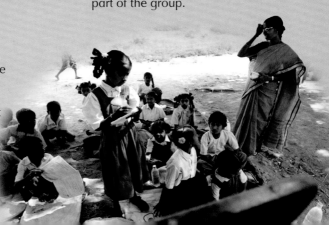

8

School bus

Children may walk or cycle to school, or go by car or bus. Often there is a special bus for school children. In snowy places they may ski or ride on a snow vehicle called a skidoo.

High-tech schools

In many schools, children have lots of things to help them learn, such as computers or books. But in some countries, children have to share books, or have no books at all.

Special schools

Some children go to special schools where they have extra lessons to learn how to dance or sing, or do sports. Other schools help people with special learning needs, such as deaf or blind people.

This is a special school for dance in Thailand.

9

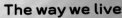

At work

People go to work to earn money so they can pay for their food, clothes and houses. Most people work only during the day, but others, such as doctors and the police, also work at night.

In an office

Today, a lot of work is done in offices. People sit at a desk with a computer and a telephone. Computers are used for all kinds of office work, from writing letters and emails, to doing really difficult sums.

Skilled worker

Some people work with their hands to make or mend things. Carpenters work with wood, plumbers work with pipes, and electricians work with electricity.

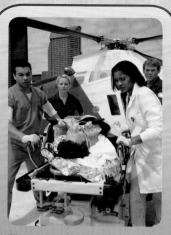

Emergency!

Police, firefighters and ambulance crews are all part of the emergency services. Their work can often help to save lives. They must always be ready to help at any time of the day or night.

Animal doctor

Veterinarians are trained to work with animals. Some vets need to understand how lots of different animals' bodies work. Other vets work with one type of animal, such as horses.

In a factory

People who work in factories make things, or put things together, such as bicycles. Some of the work might be done by hand but a lot of it is done by machines.

The food we eat

Long ago, people ate only what they could grow, catch or hunt themselves. Today, supermarkets sell food from all around the world. This means we can eat foods such as strawberries all year round, and not just when they are in season.

Preparing food

Food such as fish must be cleaned carefully ready for cooking. This fish has had its head, tail, scales and bones cut away. The fleshy parts that are left are called fillets.

Steaming

In New Zealand, there are lots of hot springs and steaming geysers. These underground water sources are naturally hot. The Maoris use the water to cook their food and keep it warm.

12

Eat in, take away

Today, people cook at home less often. We can go out to eat in a café or restaurant. Or we can buy take-away foods, such as pizza or burger and chips, to eat almost anywhere.

Cooked over a fire

In some areas, people do not have electricity or gas. They cook meals in a big pot over an open fire. It can take hours to collect the firewood.

Based on rice

In eastern countries, many meals include rice. Rice can be steamed and served with a hot, spicy curry, or made with milk and sugar into a pudding. In fact, some people eat rice for breakfast, lunch and dinner.

Did you know?

One of the most costly foods is caviar. It is the tiny black eggs from a large fish called a sturgeon. The best caviar costs more than a new bicycle. It tastes very salty.

Bony bits

Your bones are strong
and hard. They hold up
the softer parts of your
body. Your muscles
move your bones. All of
your bones together are
called your skeleton.

Bone shapes

Different bones have
different shapes. The
longest bone is your
upper leg, or thigh bone.
The widest bone is your
hip. The main bone inside
your head is your skull.

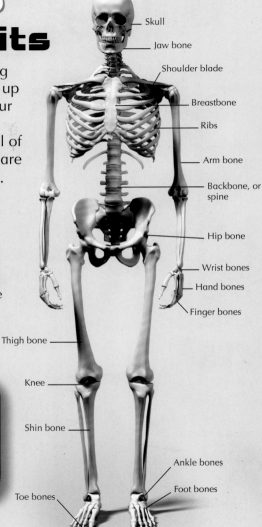

- Skull
- Jaw bone
- Shoulder blade
- Breastbone
- Ribs
- Arm bone
- Backbone, or spine
- Hip bone
- Wrist bones
- Hand bones
- Finger bones
- Thigh bone
- Knee
- Shin bone
- Ankle bones
- Foot bones
- Toe bones

Did you know?

A young baby has
about 350 bones. As
it grows, some of the
bones join together. This
is why an adult has only
206 bones.

14

Hip joint

At the point where your thigh meets your hip there is a joint called a ball joint. This allows the thigh bone to move in almost every direction.

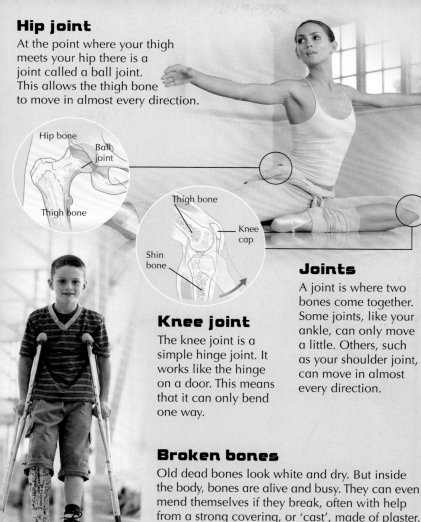

Hip bone

Ball joint

Thigh bone

Thigh bone

Knee cap

Shin bone

Knee joint

The knee joint is a simple hinge joint. It works like the hinge on a door. This means that it can only bend one way.

Joints

A joint is where two bones come together. Some joints, like your ankle, can only move a little. Others, such as your shoulder joint, can move in almost every direction.

Broken bones

Old dead bones look white and dry. But inside the body, bones are alive and busy. They can even mend themselves if they break, often with help from a strong covering, or 'cast', made of plaster.

Muscles

Every time you move, you use your muscles. Even when you are sitting still, your muscles are busy working. You are still breathing and blinking, and your heart carries on beating. All of these actions use muscles.

Shoulder muscle

Arm muscles

Powerful muscles

Muscles come in all shapes and sizes. Some muscles are large and powerful. Lifting weights can make your muscles stronger.

Did you know?

You have hundreds of muscles in your body – in fact, about 640. Your muscles make up almost half your body weight.

The biggest muscle is in the buttock (bottom).

Muscle power

Most muscles are joined to a bone at each end. When the muscle gets shorter, it pulls on the bones and makes your joints move. Usually several muscles pull together for each movement.

The large muscle in your lower leg is called the calf muscle.

The smallest muscle is inside the ear.

The longest muscle is across the front of the leg.

Tireless legs

Athletes who run long distances have longer, thinner muscles than weightlifters. These muscles may not be so big, but they can keep working for much longer. This helps the athletes to run long races without tiring.

Face it

You have more than 60 muscles in your head and around your eyes, nose and mouth. You use these to make your face move. Try looking surprised, happy or sad. Can you feel the muscles working?

17

On the outside

Your skin covers your body all over. It helps to protect you from small knocks and scrapes, germs and the harmful rays of the Sun. And when your skin does get cut or scratched, it even repairs itself.

Fingerprints

The skin on your hands is covered with lines and creases that help you to hold things tightly. These lines make up little patterns. The ones on your fingertips are called fingerprints. What's amazing about these is that every person's fingerprints are different.

Waterproof

Your skin stops water from getting into your body when you go swimming. But it does let water out through tiny holes called pores. We call this sweating and it helps to cool you down.

Different colours

Skin comes in lots of different colours, from dark to light. People who live in hot, sunny countries often have darker skins. Darker skins help prevent skin from burning.

18

Your skin

The tough outside layer of your skin is actually dead. Bits rub off all the time. But new skin is always growing too. Hairs grow through the skin. They are attached to nerves to help you feel things.

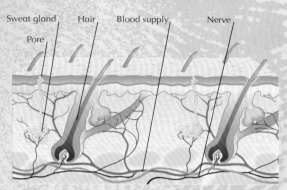

Sweat gland   Hair   Blood supply   Nerve

Pore

Your hair

You have hair all over your body. The tiny hairs on your arms help you feel things. The hair on your head keeps you warm. The colour of your hair, and whether it is straight, curly or wavy, will depend on what your parents' or grandparents' hair is like.

Wavy red hair

Straight blonde hair

Straight brown hair

Curly black hair

Breathing

What do you do all the time, yet hardly ever think about? You breathe – in and out, all day and all night. This is because your body needs a gas called oxygen, which is in the air all around you.

Breathing in, breathing out

As you breathe in, air flows into two spongy bags in your chest called lungs. Your lungs take in the oxygen from the air and release the waste carbon dioxide gas, which you breathe out.

Puffer

People with an illness called asthma often need to use an inhaler, or puffer, to help them breathe more easily.

Your lungs are like two balloons that fill with air when you breathe in.

Air

You need to breathe air all the time. So if you swim under water you either have to hold your breath or breathe through a tube called a snorkel.

 Snorkel

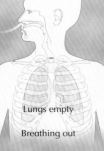

Windpipe

Lungs

Lungs full

Breathing in

Lungs empty

Breathing out

Voice box

When you talk, sing or shout, you use your voice box. Air coming up the windpipe from your lungs shakes the voice box to make the sounds. Opera singers train their voices so they can sing loudly.

The lungs

You normally breathe in and out through your nose. As you breathe in, the ribs in your chest move upwards and outwards. Air passes down your windpipe and fills up your lungs. When you breathe out, your chest moves downwards and inwards, pushing the air out of your lungs.

Blood

Blood flows all around
your body. Pumped by
the heart, it never stops
moving. Its main job is to
carry oxygen, and special
substances from food, all
around your body.

Blood vessels

Blood vessels are
the tubes that carry
blood all around
the body. Arteries
are blood vessels
carrying blood
with fresh oxygen.
Veins carry blood
containing waste
carbon dioxide.

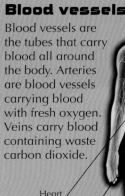

Heart

Artery

Vein

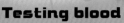

Testing blood

Sometimes when you are ill a nurse
may take a few drops of your blood
for a test. Blood often carries germs or
other signs of illness that can help a
doctor understand why you are unwell.

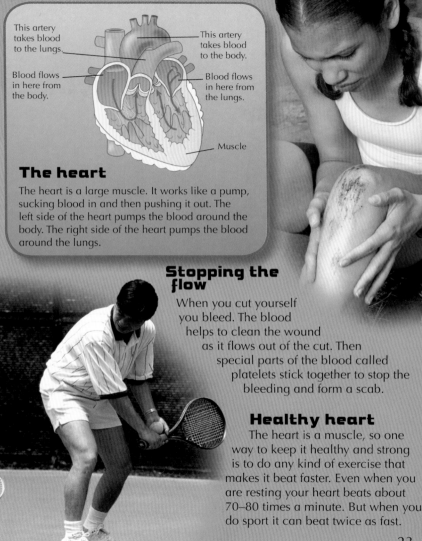

This artery takes blood to the lungs.

This artery takes blood to the body.

Blood flows in here from the body.

Blood flows in here from the lungs.

Muscle

The heart

The heart is a large muscle. It works like a pump, sucking blood in and then pushing it out. The left side of the heart pumps the blood around the body. The right side of the heart pumps the blood around the lungs.

Stopping the flow

When you cut yourself you bleed. The blood helps to clean the wound as it flows out of the cut. Then special parts of the blood called platelets stick together to stop the bleeding and form a scab.

Healthy heart

The heart is a muscle, so one way to keep it healthy and strong is to do any kind of exercise that makes it beat faster. Even when you are resting your heart beats about 70–80 times a minute. But when you do sport it can beat twice as fast.

23

Seeing and hearing

You have five senses. These are sight, hearing, smell, touch and taste. Sight and hearing are perhaps the most important. They allow you to see the world around you, and hear what is going on.

Iris   Pupil

Wide open

Light enters the eye through a hole called the pupil. The coloured part around it is called the iris. In normal light the pupil is quite small (left). In poor light the pupil gets bigger (right) so that more light is let in.

Too much noise

Your ears hear all kinds of sounds, from a quiet whisper to a huge crack of thunder. But some sounds, such as very loud music, can damage your hearing.

Did you know?

Your ears actually help you to ride a bike! This is because parts of the ear, called the semicircular canals, have nothing to do with hearing. Instead they help you to balance.

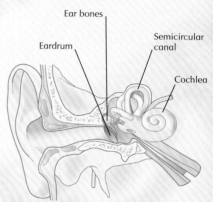

High pitched

Your ears can hear a wide range of sounds, from the very low to the very high. But, as people get older, they find it harder to hear the highest sounds. Most adults cannot hear the high-pitched squeaks of bats – but most children can!

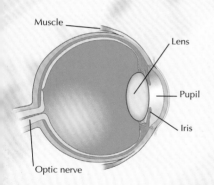

Muscle
Lens
Pupil
Iris
Optic nerve

Ear bones
Eardrum
Semicircular canal
Cochlea

Inside the eye

As light enters the pupil, a lens, just like the lens on a pair of glasses, focuses the light. This makes what you see nice and clear. The eye then sends this picture along the optic nerve to your brain.

Inside the ear

Sounds hit a piece of skin in the ear called the eardrum. They then travel through three tiny ear bones to a snail-shaped part of the ear called the cochlea. From here the sounds travel along nerves to your brain.

25

What is it made of?

Every substance, material and object in the Universe is made up of tiny particles, or bits, called atoms. There are just over a hundred different kinds of atoms. Some substances, like gold, contain only one kind of atom, but others, such as plastic, contain atoms of several different kinds.

Too small to see

A microscope magnifies things (makes them look larger). You can use it to look at the dust-like pollen from a flower, or the tiny grains of sand that make up a rock. But atoms are much too small to see, even with a microscope.

Building with atoms

Atoms are like the building bricks of the Universe. Just as toy bricks can be clipped together to make all kinds of different shapes, tiny atoms join together in different ways to make all the things we see around us – including our own bodies.

All mixed up

When you mix some substances together, you cannot separate them again. For example, if you mix coloured paints, you cannot 'unmix' them to get the original colours back.

Easy to separate

Some substances are easy to separate. If you add water to sand you get a squidgy mixture. But when sand dries out, you are left with just sand again.

Blue, yellow and red are called primary colours. You can use them to mix any colour you like.

Clothes up close

Your clothes are made up of tiny threads, or fibres, which you can see magnified here. Some are natural fibres, such as wool and cotton. Others, like nylon, are made from chemicals in factories.

Energy

Energy is the ability to make things happen, move or change. There are many kinds of energy, including light, heat, electricity and sound. One kind of energy can also change into another.

Energy for life

You need energy to run, jump, shout, breathe and even think. All your energy comes from the food that you eat. Your stomach breaks down the food to unlock the energy stored inside it.

Energy from the Sun

Heat from the Sun warms the air, land and sea. Plants use the energy in sunlight to make their own food. Sunlight can also be turned into electricity using solar panels.

This car has solar panels that make electricity to drive its wheels.

28

Food energy

Sugary foods give us instant energy. Starchy foods, such as pasta, bread and rice, release their energy more slowly, and keep us going for longer.

Movement energy

Things that move very fast, such as the wind, have a lot of energy. A wind turbine has propeller-like blades that turn in the wind. The turning blades drive a generator that produces electricity.

Fuel energy

Fuels are energy-rich substances that we burn for light and heat, and to power machinery. Coal, oil and gas are called fossil fuels. They formed millions of years ago from the remains of dead plants and animals.

An oil rig pumps oil from under the sea floor.

Did you know?

The Sun's energy makes life on Earth possible. Heat and light take just over eight minutes to travel from the Sun's surface to the Earth.

29

Solid, liquid, gas

Substances can exist in three different forms. Solids keep their shape and size. Liquids can flow and change shape, but they cannot be squeezed smaller. Gases can flow and change shape. They can also be squeezed smaller or spread out bigger.

Different water

Liquid water flows in rivers and oceans. Water also exists as solid ice, and as a gas called steam.

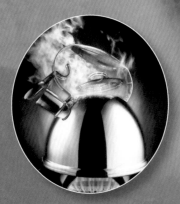

From liquid to gas

When we heat water in a kettle or a saucepan, bubbles of gas form in the water and escape as steam. This change from a liquid into a gas is called evaporation. When a gas cools and turns back into a liquid, it is called condensation.

Floating on air

Air is a mixture of gases, such as nitrogen, oxygen and carbon dioxide. Some gases weigh less than the gases in air. This airship is filled with a gas called helium. Helium is lighter than air, so the airship floats.

Airships only need small engines as they are so light.

Did you know?

If you squeeze a gas smaller, it gets hotter. This is why a bicycle pump becomes warm when you pump up a tyre.

Melt and freeze

If a solid is heated enough it will turn into a liquid. This is called melting. A glass-blower makes vases by blowing air into melted glass. When the glass cools, it becomes solid again.

This glass is so hot it glows red. Heat makes it soft so it can be shaped.

Light and colour

We can see objects because light bounces, or reflects, off them and enters our eyes. Sunlight looks white, but it is really made up of many different colours. Objects look coloured because they only reflect some of the colours in sunlight.

Single rainbows are always red on the outside, or top, of their arc.

Rainbow colours

When the sun comes out during a shower of rain, you may see a rainbow. As sunlight shines through small drops of rain in the sky, the raindrops split the white sunlight into its many colours.

Making our own light

At night and in dark places such as caves, we have to make our own light. In the past, people used candles, fires and oil lamps to see in the dark. Now we have electric light bulbs in our homes, electric street lamps and battery-powered torches.

Colour changers

Coloured lights can change the way something looks to us. Even though we know that a banana is yellow, under a blue light it reflects the light's colour and so looks blue.

Mirror image

Smooth, shiny surfaces reflect light best of all. When you look into a mirror, a window or the surface of calm water, you can see an image of yourself. This is called a reflection. This polar bear is investigating its reflection in the water.

Sound

Sounds are made when objects move rapidly to and fro. This shaking movement is called vibration. Vibrations travel through the air like ripples through water. We hear sounds with our ears.

Making music

Musical instruments have parts that vibrate to make sound. The strings of a guitar vibrate when you pluck them, and the skin on top of a drum vibrates when you hit it. When you blow into a recorder, the air inside it vibrates.

Animal sounds

When you talk, you make sound inside your throat. Many animals make sounds in their throats too. A leopard roars as a warning. A baby bird chirps to tell its parents it is hungry.

Loud and soft

The harder you bang a drum, the louder the sound it makes. If a sound is too loud it can damage your ears. This is why people who work with noisy machines wear ear covers to protect their hearing.

High and low

Some sounds are high or shrill, like a bird singing. We say that they have a high pitch. Other sounds are low and rumbling, like the boom of thunder. These sounds have a low pitch.

Pan pipes have long tubes for low notes, and short ones for high notes.

35

Simple machines

Machines make it easier for us to do things, or help us do things we could not do at all. Some of the most useful machines, like ramps, levers and wheels, are also really simple.

Ramps

Ramps are sometimes used instead of stairs or escalators. They help people to move from one level to another. They are useful for people with wheelchairs, luggage or buggies.

Gears

Gears are the toothed wheels that your bicycle chain wraps around. Usually there is one big gear wheel attached to the pedals, and one or more smaller gear wheels attached to the back wheel. Having gears of different sizes at the back makes it easier for you to ride your bicycle up and down hills.

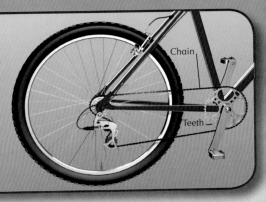

Chain

Teeth

Wheels

Wheels help us to move or carry heavy loads. Some wheels are tiny. Others are over 3 metres high. Bigger wheels make it easier for heavy trucks to travel over rough ground without getting stuck in the mud.

Screws and propellers

The screw is a simple machine. As you turn a wood screw with a screwdriver it pulls its way into the wood. A ship's propeller is also a kind of screw. But it pushes, instead of pulls, the ship through the water.

Levers

A lever can help us to lift things that would usually be too heavy for us. The see-saw is a lever that allows you to lift your partner into the air.

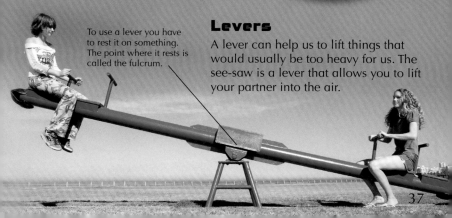

To use a lever you have to rest it on something. The point where it rests is called the fulcrum.

In the home

Kitchens have lots of machines and gadgets. They help us to prepare and cook our food. We also use machines to keep our homes and our clothes clean. Most machines are powered by electricity.

Drum

Vacuum cleaners

Vacuum cleaners use an electric motor to create powerful suction. The suction pulls the dirt and dust into the cleaner.

Dust and dirt are sucked up into this container.

This vacuum cleaner has a big ball instead of wheels to make it easier to push.

Washing machines

Washing machines have a large drum that is turned by a big electric motor. Holes in the drum let the water in and out to wash the clothes. When it is washing, the drum turns backwards and forwards quite slowly.

Did you know?

Over 100 years ago there was no electricity. People worked all their machines by hand. Imagine life without a washing machine and a vacuum cleaner.

Food processors

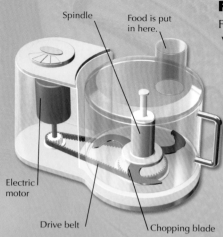

Spindle

Food is put in here.

Electric motor

Drive belt

Chopping blade

Food processors can prepare vegetables or mix ingredients much faster than can be done by hand. They have an electric motor that turns a spindle very fast. Sharp blades, for chopping, or whisks, for mixing, can then be fitted to the spindle.

Two in one

A can-opener is two machines in one. The lever part pushes the blade onto the can. The blade is a wedge that then cuts a long hole around the top of the can.

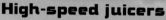

High-speed juicers

Juicers have very powerful motors. Blades chop and shred the fruit or vegetables into a soft mushy mixture called 'pulp'. The pulp is then pushed through a sieve to squeeze out all the juice.

Tools for the job

Whatever the job, from drilling a hole to making a baseball bat, there is a tool that is made to do it. Many tools are powered by electric motors – but a few still need muscle power.

Flying sparks

A grinder has a hard spinning disk that can be used to smooth, shape or cut things. When it grinds metal, sparks and sharp bits of metal fly in all directions.

Lathes

A lathe is a special machine for making shapes out of wood or metal. Baseball bats, candlesticks and bolts can be made with a lathe. To make a bat, the wood is held at one end of the lathe and spun around. A cutting tool is then held against the wood to shape it.

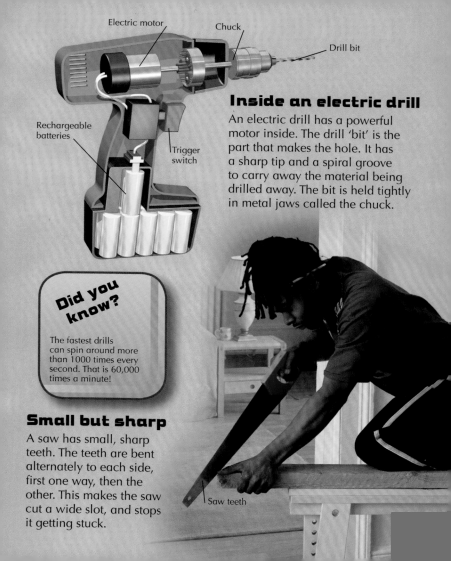

Electric motor

Chuck

Drill bit

Rechargeable batteries

Trigger switch

Inside an electric drill

An electric drill has a powerful motor inside. The drill 'bit' is the part that makes the hole. It has a sharp tip and a spiral groove to carry away the material being drilled away. The bit is held tightly in metal jaws called the chuck.

Did you know?

The fastest drills can spin around more than 1000 times every second. That is 60,000 times a minute!

Small but sharp

A saw has small, sharp teeth. The teeth are bent alternately to each side, first one way, then the other. This makes the saw cut a wide slot, and stops it getting stuck.

Saw teeth

On the farm

Farms once employed lots of people to work on the land and look after the animals. Today big machines do many of the jobs people once did. And as farms have got bigger, so too have the machines.

Plough

Ploughing time

Ploughs are like big curved spades that dig and turn over the soil in one go. They are pulled by big tractors with powerful engines. Ploughing helps to bury weeds and let air into the soil.

Milking machine

When cows were milked by hand, the job used to take all morning. Today milking machines can milk a whole herd of cows in less than an hour.

Spraying apples

Helicopters and aeroplanes are sometimes used to spray crops to keep them healthy. But many farmers are trying not to use so many chemicals, and to grow crops more naturally. This is called organic farming.

Combine harvester

A combine harvester does several jobs. First it cuts the wheat. Then it 'threshes' it, to separate the grain from the waste. The waste straw is thrown out the back as the combine moves along. The grain is stored until it can be unloaded, when it is pushed through a long tube into a trailer.

LEXION 570
Terra-Trac

The grain is stored here.

Cab

Cutter

Grain tube for unloading.

Waste straw comes out of here.

The grain is separated from the waste here.

43

On the road

Our roads are busy with machines we call vehicles. There are cars, motorcycles, trucks and buses. They take people, loads and cargoes from one place to another.

This electric car is not only quiet and clean, it also goes very fast.

Electric cars

Most cars have petrol or diesel engines. An electric car has big batteries that power an electric motor. It is quiet and wastes less energy than a petrol-engined car.

Bendy buses

Bendy buses are like two buses joined together. They can carry more people around crowded cities – but they only need one driver.

44

On two wheels

A motorbike is small and fast. But it can only carry one or two people. Some racing bikes can travel at over 300 kilometres an hour.

Articulated lorries

The biggest lorries are called articulated lorries. They have a separate cab and engine at the front, called a tractor, and a big load-carrying trailer at the back.

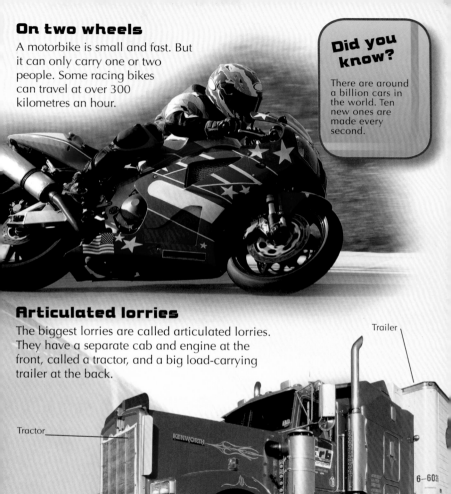

Trailer

Tractor

Index

Acknowledgements

Artwork

David Lewis Illustration: 15TR Bruce Hogarth, 17C,TL Bruce Hogarth, 18-19CRCL Bruce Hogarth, 21C Bruce Hogarth, 23TL Bruce Hogarth,25CLCR Bruce Hogarth; **Precision Illustration:** 33TL Tim Loughhead, 36BR Tim Loughhead, 39TL Tim Loughhead, 41TL Tim Loughhead, 43BC Tim Loughhead

Photography

Photo credits:
B—bottom, T—top, R—right, L—left, C—centre

Alvey & Towers: 44BR; **CLAAS:** 42-43CRCL; **Corbis:** cover TR Rob Howard, cover BR Liu Liqun, poster Bryan.Allen, 6-7C Press-Telegram/Steven Georges, 5CL epa/Robin Utrecht, 5BR Peter Turnley, 7TR Michael Wray,8TL David Turnley, 9CL Zefa/G. Baden, 10BR Stock Photos/Zefa/Lance Nelson, 11BR Louie Psihoyos, 12TL James Marshall, 12BR Wolfgang Kaehler, 13BR Liu Liqun, 14TR Reuters, 14BR Rob Lewine, 15B Zefa/Joson, 16R Zefa/Matthias Kulka,17BL Jim Craigmyle, 17TR Zefa/Gary Salter, 18BL Steve Prezant, 19R Reuters/Gary Hershorn, 20TR Roy Morsch, 20B Tom & Dee Ann McCarthy, 21TR Stephen Frink, 21BR epa/Marcos Delgado, 22CL dpa/ Maurizio Gambarini, 24BL Zefa/Mika, 28C Larry Williams, 28BL Reuters/Reuters, 28-29BRBL epa/ British Petroleum, 29TL Tom & Dee Ann McCarthy, 29R Visuals Unlimited, 30BL James Noble, 33R Zefa/Klaus Hackenberg, 35R Jonathan Blair, 36TL Zefa/Erika Koch, 36BR Charles O'Rear, 7B Zefa/Ole Graf, 37TL Lester Lefkowitz, 37CR TWPhoto, 40T Royalty-Free, 40BR Reuters, 44TL Reuters/Issei Kato, 45B Zefa/Kurt Amthor, **Dyson:** 38BL, 38TR; **Getty Images:** coverTL David Rosenberg, cover B Don Smith, coverBC Travel Ink, 1C Bill Reitzel, 4BR Robert Harding World Imagery/Upperhall, 5TR Stone/Manfred Mehlig, 6L Stone/Nicholas Prior, 7CL Stone/Lawrence Migdale, 7BR ArabianEye, 8BR Getty Image News/Robert Nickelsberg, 9TR Taxi/Gary Buss, 9BR Stone/David Hanson, 10TL Stone/Terry Vine, 11TL Photodisc Green/Ryan McVay, 11TR Photographer's Choice/Ron Levine, 13TL Reportage/Scott Nelson, 13TR Taxi/Rana Faure, 19C Image Bank/Terje Rakke, 22-23BRBL Taxi/Jim Cummins, 23TR Iconica/PM Images, 26TL Photodisc Green/Erin Hogan, 26BR Dorling Kindersley, 27TL The Image Bank/Pat LaCroix, 30C Photodisc Green/Robert Glusic, 31B Science Faction/Louie Psihoyos, 32C Aurora/Jim Thornburg, 32-33BRBL Photonica/Henrik Sorensen, 34TR The Image Bank/Joseph Van Os, 34BL Workbook Stock/Bromberger-Hoover, 35BL Stone/Robert Frerck, 36TL Taxi/Dana Neely, 41BR Taxi/Nick Dolding, 42BL Stone/Graeme Norways, 43TR Stone/Bruce Hands; **iStockPhoto:** cover BL Jerry McElroy, 2-3C Jerry McElroy, 6TL GWFlash, 8TL GWFlash, 10TL GWFlash, 12TL GWFlash, 14TL Macroworld, 16TL Macroworld, 18TL Macroworld, 20TL Macroworld, 22TL Macroworld, 24TL Macroworld, 27C Trina Denner, 31TR Charles Shapiro, 36TL Alvaro Heinzen, 38TL Alvaro Heinzen, 39TL Dan Brandenburg, 40TL Alvaro Heinzen, 42TL Alvaro Heinzen, 42TR TexasMary, 44TL Alvaro Heinzen, 45TL Andrea Leone, **L'Equip:**39BL; **Naturepl:** 25TR Hans Christoph Kappel; **Science Photo Library:** 22TR Alfred Pasieka, 24TR Adam Hart-Davis, 24TC Adam Hart-Davis, 27BR Eye of Science; **Scintilla Pictures:** 14BL John Avon